CHRONICLES OF EVERESKA

CHRONICLES OF EVERESKA
BOOK IV - DISCOVERY

TOM CAVANAUGH

Published by Spines
ISBN 979-8-89569-100-7

CONTENTS

LONG AGO, long before the breaking of the world, my people settled on the fringes of the Pegasus Galaxy. It was an area beyond the far reaches of deep space, even beyond what was called the "Sargasso Dead Zone". It was a void of space with no inhabited systems, emptiness for hundreds of thousands of light-years across. This region of space had many names from different civilizations of ages long past. Some were so ancient they had fallen, ascended, or moved on by the time we made it to their systems. We discovered many ancient cultures during our migration. The "Dead Sea" and "The Void" were some of the names I remembered from the ancient texts. Unexplored space lay behind us and "The Void" before us. It was perfect for our needs. We were newcomers to this galaxy. It was good as my father had always instructed me, "Get the 'lay of the land'," so to speak.

We had settled in this system long ago, maybe fifteen generations or more. I had seen two as a young commander after graduating from the Academy. Elder Erai lived eight to nine hundred yaren, though most averaged five to six hundred, which for many was a good life.

We had advanced healing machines, devices, our alchemy, and the mysterious ways of the **Neresturr**, who knew of processes and unknown methods of life extension. Though The Neresturr were trained enough and had the consciousness to Ascend as those who had come before us, pursued that course. Though many remained behind to continue training Lore Masters and others like themselves. There were of course legends that **Naturals**, who had specialized training and knew of esoteric processes, could attain a **Metrabolic State** involving a deep form of meditation. Their bodies hibernated, (the old timers used to say) their minds could sustain their needs somehow using consciousness and the air they breathed, only. They used quantum concepts. I had no understanding of them. There were claims of more than a score who were several hundred, if not a thousand, yaren old, that resided in caves. Most were content with their lives and passed naturally, choosing to return to the **First Place**; it was their choice as is our culture and tradition. Live, or perish, or Ascend—, all were various choices. Such was our custom to let others pursue their lives and its end, as they saw fit. Our traditions followed the principles of the Ancient Texts. "Source" or "Prime Creator", as the younger generation liked to call the "Creator" or "God", gave us the right to choose our ending as we saw fit according to each individual. Indavidualism was important. Such was the way of the "**Nupandesh**".

(STAR DATE 11-08-03/1179)

LONG BEFORE THE war had even broken out, it was many generations after we had settled here, the seventeenth, maybe more. I had been promoted to ranking commander among the youngers as I was the oldest in the group. The "Old Timers" had backed me up, over other, seasoned commanders, though I had no understanding as to why. We had established our civilization, time passed, and we traded with the few space carins who passed through this mostly unexplored region of space.

With the unexplored areas of space from which we came and the Void before us, it was mostly uninhabited. Our society had attained a state of peace, a high civilization. We were not imperialists out for conquest such as the Rogue Alliance! We thrived on exploration, discovery, creation, and wonder.

We had our military, and they excelled at combat. Their focus, though, was exploration and discovery as we sent out many teams for deep investigation. These were long-term assignments; deep space could cost a soldier two to three hundred yaren of their lives. We encouraged our youngers to seek that which was beyond, - meaning - the depths of our planet and others or examination of oceans and seas. Though, deep space was sought by many for we thrived on discovery, the wonders of new worlds, discoveries and the joy of mysteries.

It was Dusty Rhodes, the famous general, who had uncovered the lead regarding the **Ancients**, who had led us here. Time and Dimensional Travel had been contemplated even, and the Loremasters had the knowledge, mathematics, and know-how. But as the Nupandesh reveals, this was tampering with "Creator Forces" outside the realm of physicality. Such endeavors were not to be pursued lest greater evils be cast upon the entirety of the universe. They say this is how the **Wyrm** and its **Minions** entered our realm in the first place, which was the breaking of a Universal Law!

Much of this galaxy remained untouched. Even the Rogue Alliance was too distant in this region of space for us to be concerned about. They preyed primarily upon pirate outposts and such despite having spacefaring technology. They were raiders and plunderers who were simply more organized than most, which included their prey.

So when these "new people" arrived within our solar system, it surprised us. We were fully capable of repelling a would-be invasion. They were like us, explorers, and had not come for conquest. They had a level of technology and development almost on par with our own. We found it odd so much time had passed, and the few traders we interacted with had been the only lifeforms, we had seen in over a thousand yaren. So their sudden appearance was strange, though they did come from a predominantly unexplored area we had not scoped out. So we greeted them and exchanged the usual banter for future communication and trade agreements.

All of these thoughts and more ran through my mind. Memories of home seemed like many thousands of yarens ago, almost as if it had never happened. It was as if our existence had been dissolved.

"Ma'am, we have reached the outer limits of an uncharted solar system. Coming into view now," the navigator observed. "Our sensors and other telemetry have detected no signs of life," she wondered. "It's not on any of our charts or database." She looked toward me. "Even those from the space carins we trade with," she added.

"Full stop, Ensign," I commanded. "Send word have the fleet remain where they are, Ms. Jensen," I stated. "Proceed forward at impulse power.", I looked at the edges of the new system. "Let's see what we have here, Ensign," I added.

We discovered in the middle of deep space a very unusual solar system containing three stars and nine planets. The three main planets in the zone of habitation, (meaning they could sustain life). The remaining planets were devoid of any lifeforms; three were gas giants and the others were stone heaps, uninhabited.

We had just entered the system after completing the jump through hyperspace from our last location, and on the edge of it, we took our first look out the port windows at our discovery. Our long-range scanners, sensors, communications array, logistics and telemetry units were picking up on unexplained anomalies in the center of the system. Our scans were being bounced back at us, which was strange and unusual.

Upon a cursory look at some of the planets on the outer edge, we located "outposts" of one kind or another. The outer planets all had outposts, and some had mining operations on them. There had been some kind of intrusion or another as the stations in question were heaps of rubble, for the most part. Something had happened here, but long ago, and whatever had happened, we were looking at the aftermath of it.

A few of the planets looked as if they had been mined to a degree, though not extensively. Most appeared untouched for the age of the system in question. This system was very ancient, potentially billions of years old was what my science team was telling me. Strange, as there was little habitation or signs of mining or resource harvesting.

There were no transmissions of any kind coming from any of the planets. They appeared to be devoid of any signs of life, and no communications, satellites, probes, or other technologies were present.

We moved past the outer planets and into the interior of the system. The inner planets we discovered were habitable, but to our scans and sensors, no planets were registering. But we could see out the port windows, there were three planets orbiting. The largest of the three caught our attention as there seemed to be structures, which became visible only after we moved further into the system. They were undetectable to our scans and could only be seen with the naked eye. We knew this was some kind of field-damp-ening technology to jam electronic scans and sensors.

Our technicians had created similar technology, but this technology seemed to have advanced holographic proper-ties to it as well, highly sophisticated and advanced! For, the structures and the planets were invisible. A much more advanced technology than our own.

"Full stop," I ordered. "Hold position here, Ms. Jensen," I added. "Ready full exploration and scouting teams to head down to the main planet, and let's see what we have.", I inquired.

The new world we discovered had once been inhabited by an extremely advanced people. We had accessed their libraries and had learned a great deal about them in the few days of exploration here. Through study of the transcripts, artifacts, and other remnants they had left behind, they came to be known as the **Alta(n)**. They were an enigmatic people, xenophobic in their beliefs and interactions with other civilizations. The only time they assisted others outside their own was when their enemies were involved. We knew this from our records, in our database. If the civi-lization in question lacked the technological or spiritual capabilities to fend off the invaders, then they would get involved! According, to the legends and myths, they oper-ated in small groups and cells as no one had ever seen their home world!

Hence, they were mere myths and legends of ancient times, times before our time even! Like the Ancients, the **Anarue, Irda(n)**, and such, they were myths and legends. One often wondered if they were fairy tales.

But the Alta(n) were no more, according to the legends, (if they ever existed, which no one could prove). Few traders, space carins, and other civilizations we had come across through our journey from the home world, no one had ever seen an Alta(n). That is, no one who was still among the living. They were like the Ancients and such, they were no more, and as far as some considered it, they never existed!

Animal and plant life were detected, but no human life-forms of any kind were located.

There were rumors of half and quarter Alta(n), who were spread, throughout the galaxy. They were keepers of the peace. But I had never met any, and no one I knew had ever met any. The Ancient Texts spoke of them. But like so many myths contained there in, they had not been seen or heard from in well over a thousand yaren or more! They were a myth, as much of a legend as the Ancients, the **Erdue**, Anarue, and the Irda(n).

We had databases of this information along with more on the ancient past tying back to ancient times. What our Lore Masters called the "**Times, Before Times,**" well over a thousand-plus yarens ago. These myths and legends went back to the **Mother Civilization** and even our ancient beginnings that went back to the **Founder**. He had established our civilization well over a thousand plus yaren ago. But these were all legends and myths; their only proof was contained in ancient texts!

The **Word Smith**, who had revealed the knowledge of the Ancients and other teachings of the Nupandesh. She had come several hundred yaren after the Founder. She had gone on a lengthy pilgrimage and then returned. Only the Elder Erai knew where the Word Smith had gone, and they were silent. She returned to our home world, briefly speaking with the Lore Masters, and then left once again, never to be seen again. The Lore Masters shared that she had gone to seek the Mother Civilization. That was all, and beyond that, nothing more was said. Once again, that was the end of her. She was never seen or heard from again, like so much before her, was she merely a myth.

The Word Smith was like the legendary Mother Civilization; she too was a myth and legend., Like **Telaneous** and **Lady Naneth**. They were fairy tales to comfort children in times of trouble, no more! Though our ancient texts speak of her, and there are even a few Elder Erai who remembered her. I was a young lieutenant back then, fresh out of the Academy. Cadets had spoken of her, but I had to remain pragmatic and logical. I had learned, as most cadets, the basic metaphysics and even philosophy our society had been established upon, as most did. But just because you heard of a thing or person doesn't make it so!

However, when it came to existential stuff of a spiritual nature that fell into the realms of the unexplained, they were best left at the door of common sense! A commander must focus on what she can see, hear, and touch. The - "numbers of troops, ships, locations, strengths, weaknesses —"were things, which could be calculated!

I left such concepts to those who knew them best. This was why we had "Counselors and Lore Masters." That was their realm; mine was the battlefield!

There were many teachings, throughout the known Erai history. These ancient memories had fallen into archaic teachings, becoming legends which, in turn, became myths. Five generations had passed since her departure, (if there ever was one). I left such considerations to those who knew them best.

I contemplated these concepts often, in my mussings when I was on my downtime. I figured when we found a suitable planet to rebuild and settle down, as a Matron, I could entertain such ideas. Until then, I had to focus, and that meant being logical in my command.

Through replication of artwork and from their own writings, three-dimensional replicas were created of the Alta(n). We discovered the Alta(n) were roughly, five feet for females and five feet seven for males, they were short, compared to us. They were fair-skinned, with slanted eyes and usually had black hair with a (blue tinge) we had observed. We weren't sure if the "tinge" was a cultural thing or genetic. Not only were they said to be exotic, - "some would say 'Beautiful,'" - but they were extremely skilled in combat.

They had advanced technologies beyond our capabilities. They had left their entire "library" for whoever would arrive. Their accumulated technology and knowledge was contained there. The Alta(n) had apparently emerged from a wormhole from a parallel universe. Though like many things in this universe, until proven otherwise, they were myths and pure fiction made to soothe the minds of children.

The Alta(n) lived in huge megalithic cities of crystal, stone, and glass. Through some advanced method, they had learned how to fuse materials together, creating incredibly strong building materials for the architecture of their cities and living spaces. We had a system for fabrication using a similar technique, but this was more sophisticated, and they could consciously create what they visualized; we could not. The huge walls of these megalithic cities were a mile high in some places and over a mile in thickness. Our recovery teams (composed of engineers, archeologists, historians, anthropologists, and Lore Masters) were astonished at the Megaliths they beheld upon this mysterious planet of wonders.

This system of building cities made it so the Alta(n) didn't use up their land space. It also freed up the available land mass so that everyone could enjoy it. No one owned huge tracks of land. Our own culture (and most advanced civilizations like ours) had the same principles. Like the Alta(n), we too believed that we belonged to the land and no one owned it as it existed for all.

This system also made it so that the Alta(n) had more land mass for cultivating resources and creating parks, conservatories, or other projects.

(STAR DATE 6-22-04/1179)

WE HAD DECIDED to establish several colonies on the planets. The Counsel had decided that off-loading some of the civilians to set these colonies up was fair. Civilians had that choice, as was the Erai custom. Besides, they had been cooped up on the ships for several yarens since we had left our home world. Well over a hundred thousand babies had been born, during our migration. A few hundred were born during the time of the **Trials**, but that situation was different from our migration.

We had no reference as far as history went for comparison. Every man was free to pursue his life as he saw fit. Such had been our custom since our early beginnings. We had established this because of what had occurred during the time of the Trials! The civilian populace had been cooped up on these ships for many yaren during our lengthy journey. It was their choice, and so I granted the access, despite circumstances. The Counsel managed the civilian populace, though they were under military protection. But I felt it a tactical move to have some of our people relocate to these planets. They could, under these circumstances, grow and establish our civilization once more. It was worth the risk.

The Counsel had their concerns, which I let them pursue what was in their best interests. I had my own. We had assembled scores of exploration teams to further investigate the planet, more in depth. Other exploration teams were sent out to scope the other planets as well; no stone would be left unturned! Exploration drones, probes, and robotic explorers had been sent out to map the planet, take specific readings such as gravity anomalies, areas rich in resources, magnetic anomalies, etc. The more in-depth scrutiny and survey of the planet itself, was left to the exploration teams who were sent in by land, air, and water. The teams moved by boat, hovercraft, horseback, and on foot so that nothing was missed. The assignments were always lengthy, but many took them just to get away for a while. It gave an individual time to think and consider things. Remembering my days as a cadet, I took a number of similar assignments myself.

(STAR DATE 6-24-04/1179)

THE EXPLORATION TEAMS were weeks into their assignments when they made a startling discovery. Something amazing had been found, something the likes of which no one had ever seen before.

"What, repeat team five, a what?" I heard our communication officer inquiring.

"We've discovered some kind of 'Sanctuary.' The teams are not quite sure what it is. There's a 'Library' and 'Control Room.'. The Commander should come down and look at it herself, over," came the reply.

"We're not exactly sure what we're looking at. You'd better send some of the 'Lore Masters' to take a look at this stuff. We don't know what to make of it," came another inquisitive message. "Just send everyone. This place is extensive goes for miles!" the team leader exclaimed.

My counsel went over the details a few days later to put together the right team. There were already several archeological survey teams scouring the planet's surface and focusing on several ancient sites.

According to some of the teams, this region was vast and filled with ancient machinery. This machinery apparently was still in working order. Stranger still, the machines had switched themselves on and were powering up. There were plenty of automated systems, and we knew the planet was running on some kind of sophisticated 'Artificial Synthetic Intelligence.' But it too was something we were unfamiliar with. Our specialists had no idea where the central core was located., As was the case with most of the discoveries, upon this enigmatic planet. Several key archeologists, anthropologists, linguists, scholars, and engineers were pulled from other sites and deployed to the new place rather hastily.

A few days later after teams were dispatched to the location, this transmission came over the coms. "A ladder, a ladder of ascension, we got the world's highest ladder here! My god, it reaches into the heavens. You got to see this thing to even imagine it," the surveyor exclaimed over his **'ODT'**!

The messages were pouring in regarding this 'Sanctuary,' whatever it was. A ladder that climbed into the heavens, I tried to imagine what such a ladder was for. Why had the Alta(n) constructed it, and for what purpose? My mind mused and drifted off into deep thought, as I imagined climbing the ladder and making the discovery of a lifetime!

"Your orders, ma'am?" I heard the surveyor ask.

"Secure the perimeter, I'm coming out for a look at this myself," I said.

"Understood," came the reply.

I should have already been down there with the teams, but work with the Counsel and other concerns had kept me for the past couple of days. I mussed over these thoughts and others as I boarded the transport. With me, I brought another science team and more Lore Masters, It looked like between the "Sanctuary" and the "Ladder," we'd be busy.

Upon our arrival, we split up into smaller groups. Unlike most of the structures throughout the planet, which were huge, these were smaller and not so grandiose. The science team split up and had a look around. I entered the building where the ladder was erected, I wanted to take a closer look at this thing and figure out its exact purpose. This was something not typical of this planet, and we had learned a lot in the short time we had been here. One thing we had learned was that there was nothing typical, about this planet or the former inhabitants.

When I thought of a "Ladder Ascending to Heaven," I had several different ideas, but what I discovered was not as I had imagined. A non-descript modern ladder (stretching into the heavens) was what awaited me, upon my arrival. The strange looks from the members of the exploration teams were becoming commonplace.

Besides its modern configuration, the ladder, (we noted), was made out of an unidentified metal of unknown origin and composition. It did not come up on any of our data scanners from the many worlds we had discovered or traded with. Like the unidentified metal, the structure (from an engineering point of view) was using unknown and unidentified means in its construction and configuration.

We were surprised to see that whoever had built this thing was quite clever. Though it appeared as a "ladder," one did not have to climb but simply stepped up upon the first rung. The mechanism rapidly shifted the climber to the end. In what we later realized was the control room, there were strange alien crystal interfaces. We recognized the language of the Alta(n), alongside our own and another unidentified one. Days after our arrival and investigation, the system knew our language preference. The AI installed it on all systems everywhere, no programming required. They were for controlling the various "Planetary Systems," which covered the entire planet. The Planetary Systems had various and different functions and purposes. From environmental control to weather, defenses, communications, the teletransporter, many systems were controlled by the mechanisms. The machinery and the interfaces were highly sophisticated. Some of the technology was purely for experience of nature itself. From the Alta(n)'s point of view, "nature" was not something one simply looked at! They had floating lakes, streams, and rivers, (for example)—, which initially we didn't understand its purpose. The Alta(n) didn't want one to just see and hear nature but experience it in a way that had meaning and purpose, again using these Planetary Systems. This was an advanced form of "Earth-based" technologies of an unknown inception.

There were displays and interfaces everywhere, all of an unidentified crystal fabrication. Once again the written language of the Alta(n), our own, and the unidentified language flashed across the screens.

There were also strange devices and systems that were online but idling, as if waiting for someone to access the system. These unknown technologies we were unsure of them.

We had come across many places in our travels, but nothing here resembled them. Some of our men tried to compare this stuff to other planets we had investigated. I had to remind the teams to do away with the practice. Nothing upon those planets came close, to what we had here! The Alta(n) were advanced over our own knowledge, but they had obviously had help from someone more advanced than themselves, with this planet and its various projects. The Library had no answers to those questions.

The technology that surrounded us was of a source and level of knowledge beyond what we discovered upon the surface. All the interfaces, control panels, and displays were all of the strange crystalline fabrications with unusual and unidentified alien languages. Again what we found here did not resemble anything from the surface.

Though the interfaces and control systems displayed our language, we had no idea what they did, so they were left in their idling position until we knew what we were dealing with. It took our Lore Masters, (with the assistance of the Librarian), some time to retrieve the data from the archives.

Some of the strange displays showed other worlds in other galaxies (we assumed). We did not recognize any of the galaxies or systems as once again they were as unknown to us, as the Alta(n) were.

Since we were in an uncharted and unfamiliar region of space, all of it was a revelation. We had lost contact with the rest of the fleet and were unsure of our location after we had made the jump.

I looked at the team members, then at the ladder.

"Guess it's going to be a long climb. See you at the end," I said. I touched the ladder and planted my foot upon the first rung. No sooner did I plant my foot upon the first rung, than I was instantly transported to the end of the ladder.

I was greeted with cheers, laughter, and several comments from some team members who waited for my arrival.

Welcome, this is 'Eve.'", One of the Lore Masters waved his arm at the massive structure I gazed upon. "My god, what is this?" I was floored by what I beheld!

The massive structure floating in a containment system was a thousand times larger than our "**LDL**s," which housed thousands within them!

From what we had read on the history of "Eve," was that the "Alta(n)" had constructed these "Mechanisms" (as they were being called) roughly 2.5 billion years ago using an unknown and unidentified fabrication method with a combination of (carbon crystal) and unknown alloys in the manufacturing process. Though this "Eve" was different from its predecessors. What the "differences" were, we had no idea as there were no "originals" to compare to.

The "Alta(n)" had applied not only the latest in their technology but adapted several unknown systems into its construction and design, creating a composition of both known and unknown systems. "Eve" contained weapon systems, drive and guidance systems, telemetry, etc., all of an unknown origin and design. Once again, we found ourselves dealing with technology, machinery, and devices which were unfamiliar to us. Once again we were forced to return to the library, to bone up on all the technology and systems that had been built into this "Mechanism". We still had no idea what its purpose was. Why did the "Alta(n)" build such a thing?

My focus was the battlefield as a floating/flying city could be the edge to potential victory over the enemy. An enemy which our almighty fleet had merely resisted in the past. We never won battles but merely staved off utter defeat and loss, was all. But 'Eve' could be the final solution to end this war once and for all, was my calculation.

A HANDFUL of days had gone by, and we were still at a loss as to what we had discovered. The more we investigated, the more we found, but each find only brought more questions, than answers.

Our databases were full of yarens of research and revelations of the worlds we had found in our own galaxy. There was more data from the yarens of our journey from the home world to here we were still going over. But nothing matched what we had found here nor what was displayed on some of the screens.

The Alta(n) must have realized something like this could occur. One of our teams reported something had been activated during our initial inventory of the control room and data was being transmitted across the strange displays and interfaces. The very information we needed to make heads or tails of the technology at our fingertips, was being transmitted in our language, to our ODTs.

No sooner had that started than the alarm went off in the main control room. I headed down there since I was close and on my way anyhow. I entered and found an assembly had begun just as the message flashed across my ODT.

As I grabbed some nau'tea, I had a look at the gathering., "Commander Lissitte and Lieutenant Littrell, along with Devon Margalen, were already seated at the table. I looked at the message on my ODT as the doors opened, and Commander Trey, Captain Willis, and Spheres entered. Dusty Rhodes and Captain Carter had called the meeting. Strange as Dusty was a civilian and Carter had arrived from the rest of the fleet only recently. I took my seat as Dusty and Carter along with Sergeant Patrell and a security team entered the room escorting a middle-aged man wearing glasses.

Captain Carter took a seat next to the middle-aged man as security took a step back. They remained standing. Dusty stepped forward. "I call this meeting to order," he began.

"Everyone, this is 'the "Maker."' He's the guy who designed and built "Eve" along with many of the systems we've been studying these past months. Since he revealed himself to me and I still hold the senior rank, I called the meeting." he smiled. He looked toward me and smiled, "I didn't call the meeting to usurp the 'Commander," as she is a fine leader. I merely did it to eliminate all the questions and pomp and circumspance," he added.

"This guy doesn't need an introduction," he added and several people laughed at the comment. He took a bow and seated himself.

The Maker stood up and began, "Though the Alta(n) called me 'The Maker' in the Erai tongue, you can call me "Leon." He poured himself a cup of nau'tea and smiled at me.

"Welcome, Leon. Thank you.", I smiled and looked at Dusty and continued. "Thank you, General, for calling the impromptu meeting and assembling a fine group for it." I clapped and smiled at the group. "Here, here," I heard from a few of the attendees," along with cheers, a few whoops, and Dusty's howl as some of the men got to their feet and clapped. The women remained seated.

After the ruckus settled, I continued. "Leon, can you begin by telling us, where you have been all this time?" I inquired.

"Yes, Commander. When the Alta(n) left the planet, there was a reboot of the entire planetary system, as well as a reset of subsystems. This caused the security system to go into a temporary lockdown measure. I was caught in a stasis field, which is one of the defense mechanisms", he explained. "When your team entered the main planetary grid control, that disengaged the lock mechanism, which allowed me to get free of the infernal contraption," he exclaimed!

There were a few chuckles, gasps, and giggles. After everyone settled down, I asked the obvious question. "Do you know where the Alta(n) went," which brought on a standing ovation, more whoops, and cheers? Once they settled down again, I added, "Can you show us?" I added. This exchange brought on another uproar. Where the former inhabitants went and why was the second best thing in need of answers!

Sadly to our dismay, Leon's reply was not what we expected.

"I'm sorry, Commander," he began. "I asked to stay behind to be here with my 'Eve.' I could never abandon her", he exclaimed. "This is my creation. I had no interest in following them through some wormhole," he added. He concluded, "Been through one wormhole, you've been through them all." He laughed.

"Leon, do you know why they left?" Captain Carter asked. "Why build such as this," he waved his arm, meaning the entire planet as he chose his words and added, "simply to abandon 'Paradise' in my eyes, Leon. It doesn't make sense!" he concluded.

Leon finished his tea and poured a glass of water. He sipped. "Of course, Captain, but it may not be as paramount or extraordinary as one may conceive." He smiled. "Their work was done, and so they left. One does not need such revelations when your man would have the answers you seek.

Would you know him, one from another?" Leon smiled.

The perplexed looks of the assembly didn't take me by surprise. But I wanted to follow up on that and could see Devon was already forming a question. Leon took to his feet before anyone could follow suit. "My friends, you already have the answers you seek, there is no mystery here but only what one makes of it. There'll be more to share soon enough, but I need check on something." With that statement, he touched something on his wrist and vanished.

After everyone settled down, I got to my feet.

"I guess we'll find out what that's all about soon enough," I said. "We do need contingencies once we find out how he did that. For now, we press on, does anyone disagree?" I scanned the assembly.

I tapped my ODT.

"I have made some adjustments to our work schedules, which are as follows: Dusty, I want you and Spheres to take over training our new flight crews including command and control, along with the fighters. Commander Trey, I want you to take over production operations and resource harvesting. I've ordered three new crews to be added as I want the assembly work done night and day, Commander. If more teams are needed, let me know.

Commander Lissette, you will take over ground defense training and system security. I added two new teams. Double our efforts there, Commander.

Captain Carter, coordinate with Captain Willis. It's in your briefs, which I have updated. I want you to return to the **Repulsar** and meet with the rest of the fleet. It won't be long before the enemy learns of our ruse. Captain Willis will bring you up to speed. You are all dismissed."

I went over to the bar and poured myself a shot. "Devon, Lieutenant Littrell, remain," I ordered. Turning to Sergeant Patrell. "Sergeant, locate the Maker and have him see our team here." I waved toward Littrell and Devon. "I'm confident you can locate him," I added. Tugging on his sleeve, I whispered, "We also need to know how he pulled off that vanishing act." I added. "I gotcha." He winked. "I'm on it, Commander." He turned and exited along with the security detail.

Devon got up and poured a cup of tea. Littrell shot a look at her. "I'll have one as well." she smiled. Littrell returned to her post at the port window. I took a seat at the table, looking into my glass as I swirled the liquid within. "I think Leon's answer about 'Eve' was more than just about that flying city." I looked toward Devon," then continued. "I think Leon meant the entire planet," I concluded. "I feel you are correct about that, Commander. There was no deception, only love, earnestness, and a sense of devotion and, not just for 'Eve' but for this planet. It is like Leon is in love with it, like a parent has feelings for a child, not as a 'lover,'" she explained.

"That would explain his, - 'my creation' - comment," Littrell added. "That would also conclude they didn't return to some 'wormhole,' as he stated, through some wormhole, which feels like an assumption or forgone conclusion," Littrell explained.

I laughed, then took a sip. Devon giggled herself. "Why, Lieutenant, seems you have a knack for being an 'intuitive'. I didn't think you had a feel for being a Counselor, Lyra," Devon observed.

Littrell chugged her tea down in one gulp. "No, Devon, I'm merely the cheering section for our leader." She smiled at Devon, as her eyes slid over me back to Devon's grin.

I certainly wasn't about to let the conversation get into feelings. They were not relevant to the battle plan and figuring things out no matter how one felt about a thing or person. I gulped my drink down and squirming at the table I poured another and sat down.

"What do you think Leon was alluding to with his comment about the Alta(n) work being 'done?'" I wondered.

"I wondered about that myself, Commander," Devon admitted. "How did it relate to his 'your man and knowing one from another, comment?'"she added.

"What 'one'? There are no 'Alta(n)' in the ships databases as far as I know", Littrell added. I know those records. I helped Lissette and Patrell set them up days after we left."

"Leon is not 'Alta(n),' but I think we're missing something here," Littrell added. "Could he have meant there may have been some technology or method for beating the 'DNA Scan?'"" Littrell explained?

Lyra went back to looking out the port hole for answers, and Devon took to looking into her glass for solutions. "That would be assuming a half or quarter 'Alta(n)' had slipped aboard one of our ships," she concluded.

"It's late. We should call it a night." " my father used to say the cooler head prevails." I realized our chat had many conclusions and tangents. "We'll pick this up another time," I added.

(STAR DATE 9-2-04/1179)

DAYS TURNED into weeks and weeks into months as scores of our best engineers, scientists, archeologists, historians, linguists, and other specialists crawled over every inch of "Eve" looking for clues. Any and all related material that was subject to it was collected, cataloged, and stored in the database for our access. Needless to say, we were engrossed in its study. The "Chroniclers" and "Lore Masters" had different ideas and theories they wanted to investigate.

We had returned to the "Library" as all the data we needed relevant to "Eve" (it's study and investigation) was stored in the library computer. Everything about the planet and its multitude of systems was also loaded into the library computers as well. Much of which was spewing out loads of data on this "Unknown Mechanism" of which our crew was spending vast quantities of time studying and learning about.

One of the devices contained within the Library featured a crystal orb display. Upon command would either show information upon a flat-screen display or in 3D. This was useful we found when looking at complex systems and machinery, as visual learning was an easy way to train people. The crystal orb display was tied into a "Universal Translator," or "Librarian," as we came to call him. The Librarian featured audio and visual files, along with "3D schematics and plans." The Librarian would virtually show us the vast areas of Evereska (the Mechanism) or the associated locations attributed to the system. They were revealed upon appropriate screens for viewing and study.

The Librarian reacted and interacted with visitors to the room. Through various sensor systems built within the confines of the room as well as commands or prompts entered into the computer. It was highly sophisticated, complex, intricate and intuitive (as with all "Alta(n)" technology), we had discovered in past excursions.

The Librarian interacted through telepathy and a special interface through small crystal spheres or display panel. The Librarian was able to assimilate, collate, and compile data and appropriate records and related data accordingly. Multiple users within the Llibrary could access and interact with the system as well.

Visitors could either interact with the system through displays, virtual reality, or in 3D as much of the information was complex. We used all the systems for our investigation and study into this amazing planet, its Planetary Systems, and, of course, Evereska!

We discovered that in the immediate area of our current location, there were twenty-one sites of interest defined as: "conservatories, preserves, havens, monasteries." - of which

(Conservatories), we came to learn, were - "places of study and learning" (Preserves,) - "places for reflection and contemplation" (Havens,) - "places for creative design, conceptualization, research or study," and. (Monasteries) - were places for "instruction and training."

So these were the definitions the computer was spewing out at us as we waited, reading, studying, discussing, this new knowledge and data we were recovering from the Librarian.

Many of us preferred printed material over digital versions. We were happy to learn that the "Alta(n)" preserved their history and heritage in museums located throughout the planet. We located 'replicators' and created books and other materials essential for our missions.

The site where Eve was located was in an area we named the "Vale." The Vale was a woodland area nestled between two mountain ranges.   In the area was the Lladder of Ascension and the Library.

Prevalent throughout the region was some kind of unidentified Alta(n) technology. This unknown technology was everywhere, built into the planet itself in some places though hard to distinguish if one did not know what to look for. It was Advanced Earth Tech but of an origin we had never encountered before. The Alta(n) had created (floating rivers, streams, floating walkways, bridges, sanctuaries, refuges), and other strange manners of tech applied in a way we did not understand upon our arrival. We had thought it "natural" initially, until the Librarian informed us of the level of technology the "Alta(n)" had attained. Then we knew the truth—, all of it had been created by them, built by them.

But for what purpose?

As to that question and more, my team, consisting of Lieutenant Littrell, Sergeant Patrell, and his team, along with Spheres, Dusty, and Commander Trey, were all teaming over heaps of books, schematics, and records strewn across the conference table as we studied the information.

We were concerned as there had been some engagements with the enemy in another sector. It was apparent our diversion had led the enemy away from this sector of space. We could take a breather, but a lot of work remained as there were vast amounts of data to study and learn.

(STAR DATE 1-11-04/1179)

SEVERAL MILES from Commander Trey's operations were some ruins that had been located. Lieutenant Littell myself, and several other recovery specialists were deployed to check them out immediately. An escape pod from a freighter had been located, that meant there was someone here who may have answers.

We set out on hovercycles arriving at the outskirt of the ruins early in the afternoon. After parking, we set out on foot. While examining the site, we noticed a cave not far away which we decided to investigate.

Lieutenant Littrell myself, and three of our support personnel entered the cave as the rest of the party examined the nearby ruins.

Inside the cave, we discovered it was relatively small, with a larger recess in the back where some old bones and debris revealed the cave had been used by some animal from the planet's past, a carnivore from the evidence.

"I'm picking up strange electromagnetic readings and gravity fluctuations, ma'am," Jynx, one of the support personnel, reported to me. "The readings appear to be coming from the ceiling or the rear." As she continued, she looked to the rear and back toward the ceiling, perplexed.

"Which is it, the ceiling or the rear?" I asked.

"I'm not sure, ma'am," came her reply, followed by, "The readings keep jumping like there is some kind of interference," Jynx replied. She looked once more at her "ODT - (which is a tool used for taking measurements and examining different phenomena like electromagnetic energies, gravity anomalies, strange electrical, or associated weather phenomena). The system measures and calibrates the readings according to the user interface.

"Sounds like a hologram, a sophisticated one by the looks of it," came Lieutenant Littrell's reply.

She focused her own ODT at some nearby rock, and suddenly a display appeared.

"I think this is the master system for the entire grid here. Lyra you're a genius!" I exclaimed. "Drinks are on me tonight. We'll have nau 'tea," I exclaimed, excited about the discovery.

By interfacing through our ODT, we accessed the Librarian, who brought us up to speed on the fundamentals of the system.

All the Alta(n) wore a special pendant that was tied into this global system used for transport, among other things. The system had a platitude of different capabilities including monitoring the location of the user (for accidents and calamities) so rescue workers could quickly find injured or stranded explorers. The system gave the user useful information on location and local or regional weather, temperature, and for accessing different interfaces all over the planet.

We modified our ODT, tying it into the main computer in the library, so we had continual access to all the data for ongoing operations throughout the area.

It was late in the afternoon when we exited the cave, that Lieutenant Littrell picked up a reading of another life-form, and it was closing fast with another reading behind the first contact.

"Hey, guys, we got company. To the northeast," Lyra shouted as she pulled her sidearm.

I scanned the horizon for any sign of life. I could see in the distance a bipedal form, (human by the looks of it) being pursued by a large carnivore. The animal, resembling a saber-toothed tiger, was closing fast through the hazy dust cloud the ruckus stirred up. The female, fleeing for her life, closed in on our position, taking cover behind a boulder as the beast lunged at her. Lieutenant Litrell moved to the right side to flank the attacking carnivore as I took aim and let fly several shots from my sidearm. At the same time, Lyra took position and firing upon the animal as well. The charging carnivore came to a rushing halt, stirring up more dust in its wake, before falling over.

The first thing I noticed about our visitor was that she had the most stunning and exotic look I had ever seen. Her dress was of an unidentified and exotic nature. It was an enigma, out of place, and not native, nor was she Alta(n).

She said something in an unidentified language.

"The ODT does not recognize her language, ma'am," came Jynx's reply. She was sitting close to the girl, examining her and tending to cuts and scrapes.

The young lady switched to a "Universal Sign" language known among many different peoples. For lack of interpreter, the sign language was used across the span of the galaxy and beyond.

She introduced herself as "Anayla". She had been (up until a week ago), a slave on her way to the pens to be sold. The planet was not far from this sector of space. It was a trading colony of slavers and scavengers mixed with other explorers and intergalactic traders. So that part of her story added up. The ship had sustained damage from the asteroid belt; it was destined to crash. Anayla fled the ship in the last escape pod. Being one of the lucky survivors, she had escaped the ship, but was now alone on an alien world. She had been laying low in a ruin nearby when she heard voices and came to investigate, running into the carnivore on the hunt when our group came along.

"You are free to return with us if you wish, or we can leave you some supplies, the Erai do not hold slaves!" I exclaimed. "You can return with us," I made the invitation. Anayla nodded her head in agreement, she would be joining us.

We returned to our small base we had established by the cave. and more support personnel had arrived to investigate the area. Over the next couple days, our team was busy activating, restoring, or repairing various systems on the grid that the Librarian had informed us were essential for activation of Evereska. Apparently the systems had been shut down and deactivated when the Alta(n) had left.

Some systems were in need of repair. The activation was a hard start shorting those minor systems. The data files regarding the whereabouts of the Alta(n), why they had left, and where they went had been purged from the system. With no back up files for unknown reasons. The Librarian had no information regarding that. I informed "Commander Lisette" about the cave, to take charge and send in more teams and returned with Lyra and the rest of our team, with Anayla in tow.

I decided to question Anayla more in depth about her background. Considering no life had been found anywhere we had explored so far, it was part of the process considering her unexpected and sudden appearance. We were at war; infiltrators, spies and saboteurs were commonplace with the enemy, and we had learned the hard way! I was, (formerly), "Military Intelligence," which was my job in the early days as a cadet.

This was the protocol and process; it was how the Erai had learned to capture enemies. We employed the empaths during questioning of unknown persons. Devon was a master at it. Some suspected she was a Neresturr, though she herself did not claim such a thing!

I noticed Anayla had assembled various crystals and stones she had found during her exploration of the planet. She was fiddling with some unidentified tech, oblivious to the onlooking group.

After carefully observing Anayla, I noticed she did carry herself with confidence though she "appeared to be an obedient and willing slave". Something about not her story, but her, didn't add up.

She moved like a cat and had grace. Her build and form was one of an athlete, a trained specialist, or an assassin. Though she feigned klutziness or, more so, awkwardness, it seemed an act, a very well-disguised act. Her injuries, as she claimed, had been inflicted from abuse as a slave, but they looked more like battle scars than from abuse and neglect.

"Anayla, can you set that tool down for a moment?" I asked.

I stood up, and Anayla followed suit, looking inquisitively like a "good slave," head slightly bowed.

"We investigated the wreckage, Anayla. Looks as if you couldn't have gotten out of there, without some help?" I inquired. Before she could reply, I continued, "You got out of that ordeal on your own? Quite a feat for a simple, slave girl," I asked, looking into her eyes for honesty or duplicity.

"I guess I got lucky," Anayla exclaimed, feigning a forced smile.

"Maybe, Anayla, may be," I continued. Nodding at Lieutenant Littrell was the signal. Lyra pulled one of her carbon steel throwing knives and hurled it rapidly at Anayla. The girl dodged the sleek blade just knicking her arm. To an untrained, slave girl or civilian, the attack would have been lethal, severely injuring the target. Anayla got into a fighting stance and then reset, realizing she had blown her cover. She ran her hand through her hair.

"Enough," I called, "the game is up, Anayla. We know

you're not a peasant, slave girl, but what exactly you are we will discover." I demanded from her.

Anayla relaxed and let her guard down, returning to her previous position. She regained her composure, looking serene and meek.

"Until you tell us more, you're considered an enemy. We don't know who you really are and cannot jeopardize our mission here," I commanded. "You will not be permitted to leave until we get the truth. Take her to the detention facility if there is such a place," I commanded the guards who had entered during the fruckus.

"That's unfortunate," Anayla replied as the guards ushered her away. As she exited, she added over her shoulder, "I'm not here for you. Didn't even know anybody was here." She was puzzled.

Once everyone had cleared, Lyra poured herself a drink and sipped as we conversed.

"How did you know she was not a slave girl?" Littrell asked, looking toward me, then back out the window, perplexed about something.

On the "surface," Lyra appeared as a "conformist." Though conservative in the traditional sense, Littrell was related to the old families. They rose after the "Trials" and did follow many of the customs and traditions most conformists' families adhered to. Though it was unorthodox to join the military at such a young age. Most conformists looked forward to working and starting a family at this age when they were still young. Though this was at a time when things were different, many of the rules and such no longer applied.

Littrell could have easily gone into the "Leadership Caste." It is from this group "Counsel Members" are groomed and brought into the civilian leadership within the "Conformist Party."

Littrell could certainly work toward a leadership position, within the party! Her ancestry and background assured a stout career there.

She was the niece of the famous "Commander Blake." He went on to lead the party during the time of the "Trials". Though Blake could have been "Commander" or even Prime Minister." Blake led the civilian arm of the party, he chose another path and left the military shortly after the conflict ended.

The war hero turned to the spiritual path and had quite the following. Despite his following and prestige, Blake had disappeared shortly after the "Trials" had ended. He had taken on a "Scientific Excursion and Expedition" of some sort. He was never seen again and was assumed dead.

His team had entered a region of space called the "Dark Sea." It was a part of "The Void". It was a fringe area bordering a sector of space, within the region that was unexplored. A virtual no-man's land. Most who had entered, never returned! There were no known systems within this region, that along with hostile space aliens, pirates, and slavers. The few space carins we traded with, along with hearty explorers avoided this region of space.

Most avoided the area, so it was left unexplored and ignored. It was part of the "Sargasso or Dead Sea" as many called it. Only the bold and daring entered, though I deemed them foolish as they were never seen or heard from again! The few that did return from there refused to speak of their experiences (which was their right), and the few that had documented their experiences the files had been sealed by the Lore Masters for unknown reasons. Our legends spoke of it, and the Nupandesh explained, this region of space was to be avoided as no one had ever successfully reached the other side!

I had to laugh at the bitter irony of it all. Because the very region of space that was to be avoided is where we found this planet.

I wasn't sure about Littrell's angle. I wondered, considering her devotion to the military. Conformists made good soldiers. They just didn't like to fight unless they had no diplomatic solution! Littrell was no exception. She had aspired and moved through the ranks as a favorite and had a promising career. Yet she was still just a "Lieutenant" and had not taken a promotion, nor had she pursued one for some time now.

I wondered about her as I knew she had to have some kind of angle to restore the face her family had lost. When Blake had gone on his mission, much had been lost to her family. He had been warned it was a 'Fool's Errand;' the other families mocked them! When he failed to return, face was lost, and the family lost much power within the leadership caste.

Lyra had often thought our leader at the time the war broke out was too soft on the enemy. That had it been "Blake," who should have been "Prime Minister". He would have acted and done so sooner. There were always those out there who wanted and theorized that they would have done things differently. It was the guilt of the day we all failed, but many carried more than their share of it. Some, possibly "Littrell," carried shame at the loss of the home world. They continued to punish themselves daily for our planet's failure on that fateful day!

I'd had my fill of it, but realized I was a young captain at the time. Despite being in charge, I loathed it sometimes as my decisions led to my comrades' potential deaths. Such was the life of a military leader. This was "duty and obligation;" despite how I felt, feelings in this situation had to be set aside for the good of the fleet.

I smiled at Lyra. We had grown up together and had entered the Academy after finishing school. We were best friends, beyond comrades in arms. We had a bond that extended beyond the military as we were like sisters considering our history.

I answered Lyras question with one of my own, "You were the one who came to me, Lieutenant, with your concerns and observations. What made you feel she was not as she said she was?" I inquired.

I already knew the answer. I just wanted to hear it from her. I knew the conclusions of where this line of logic would lead. Hearing it from her, would only validate and verify my own reasoning and conclusions.

"Anayla's story didn't add up. I've never heard of slavers heading that far out into uncharted space. Considering there's nothing out here. That didn't make sense," she observed. Continuing she added, "Of all the space charts from the trade ports and explorers we copied data from, no one, slavers included, heads out into this vector of space. No one does. Even pirates, or the Rogue Alliance, tend to avoid this area," she exclaimed. Pausing for a moment, she sipped her drink and gathered her thoughts, she continued. "I also noticed her 'scars.   They could have been from years of abuse as a slave, but some of them were obvious battle injuries from being on the lines. There's a big difference between 'battle injuries' and what she may have sustained from neglect and abuse," Littrell added.

"Those were obvious revelations she could not hide. Neither could she hide her grace, her form, her ability." She paused choosing her words carefully. "These were 'tells, revealing who and what she really was, which was not a 'peasant slave girl' as she claimed. She was good, but not that good and had been caught." She poured another glass and drank heavily. "Much of what I know I attribute to what I've learned from you, ma'am." She grinned at me. "Your training, experience—, it's paid off in many ways!" she exclaimed. She shot me a smile and added, "The woman I've become today I owe to you. You got me through all of this, and for that I'll always be grateful." she added!

(STAR DATE 1-17-04/1179)

OVER THE COURSE of ninety days, the Maker showed us many new technologies and applications available on the planet-wide system. We learned about the "Tele-transporter System", more on the power systems, manufacturing, fabrication, and processing. We learned more about the planet-wide defenses, communications, logistical systems. It was all highly advanced beyond our knowledge.

What surprised us was the Maker's extensive knowledge, he seemed to have no limits. He perplexed some of our most talented Lore Masters as there seemed to be no limits to his knowledge. I sent Dusty Rhodes and Spheres to lend a hand as they were specialists with a wide knowledge of systems. Lieutenant Littrell and Commander Lissette threw in as well.

They had been combing over records more so than others, since we'd arrived at the Library Complex.

The day had started out gray and overcast, with a light fog hanging over the area like some kind of predetermined pall. There were those who had been trained in this; there was an actual planet-wide geoengineered weather system. If you didn't like what nature dished up, with a push of a button, one could change the weather outside with a flick of a switch!

I entered the briefing ready to flick that switch. Fog made me nervous as unsuspecting foes and potential enemies lurked around the corners ready to pounce on the unwary. But as had been the prognostication earlier, the fog burned off and cleared, just as we were all sitting down for our morning briefing.

Since our arrival to this sector of space and ongoing operations, we had set up regular routine patrols around the system. Since it was massive, there were groups that patrolled the inner and outer planets. We had learned their names from the Alta(n). The inner planets which were in the zone of habitation were "Evereska," which was the primary planet where we discovered "Eve." "Sif," which was a tiny water planet and the mid-sized, "Tigriss" which resembled our home world. "Solana" was the primary star for the system, roughly the same age as the star in our home world. The outer planets were "Ilianna," a tiny planet. The dead star "Esynia." Then came "Caliastro," the gas giant and his brother "Mastiff." On the outer edge of the system was the massive "Hyacinth," which resembled the flower, "Tarea," a young star and "Neptus".

We had even established some outposts, though hidden throughout the system for early response. Intrusion (if it were the case) would be met with early defenders, before reinforcements arrived from elsewhere. One of our LDLs, "**Raven**" commanded by Captain Carter and some support ships were on the fringes of the system, ready to respond if the need arose.

The system was a three-star sector of space with nine planets contained within it, so there was a lot of space to cover. Three of the nine planets were closer in towards the primary sun. The others much further out into the reaches of space. It was almost as if some kind of cosmic incident had removed the middle planets. If there had been any, which according to the "Maker" there never had been.

Every bit of this system was being scoured by exploration and science teams. The problem was we just didn't have enough manpower to cover it all. Even with the use of drones and robotic exploration, the system was too vast to cover, explore, and protect with our small numbers.

I was informed a small ship, a shuttle possibly or scout ship, had entered our sector of space. I would have paid it no mind, leaving it to Littrell or another. The ship in question came from the same vector of space we came from, so I looked into the matter as it became personal to me.

The ship was still far out on the fringes of the system. I sent a group that had been on patrol to intercept it and take a look at our visitor.

Lieutenant Littrell entered the control room. "Code X communique, ma'am. It's marked urgent." She wiped sweat from her brow and added, "It's from the fleet. They got the **Repulsar** underway!" She said excitedly! "Finally, some good news. I'll take it in my office," I told Littrell.

"Littrell, I want you to handle the briefing. After all, Captain Carter needs to be brought up to speed. Everyone else pretty much knows the latest.", I commanded.

"Ma'am?" Littrell seemed puzzled.

"You have a question, Lieutenant?" I asked.

"Permission to speak frankly?" Littrell inquired.

"Go ahead," I said.

"A lead 'Officer' usually runs a briefing, Ma'am." She shrugged her shoulders, caught off guard by the order. "Traditionally speaking, higher-ranked officers are usually briefed by someone of their rank or higher," she smirked as she looked my way, confused.

"'Traditionally' yes, but considering the circumstances, Lieutenant, I think we can skip the protocols," I confirmed. Littrell cracked an awkward smile. "I have confidence in you, Lieutenant. Don't let 'Carter' intimidate you. He's warm and fuzzy on the inside," I added with a smile.

Littrell smiled, and then we both laughed. Though 'Carter' was a bear of a man, his nickname out of the Academy had been 'Honeybear' as he was a soft touch.

I entered my office and sat down, as I noticed Sergeant Patrell at a workstation nearby.

"Sorry, ma'am." He hesitated, then added, "Thought I'd be done by now." He smiled.

I was puzzled for a moment, then remembered I had made it where some protocols, specifically security, had to be logged on one of my office computers. Patrell was in charge of 'security,' so his presence was expected. It was taking some adjusting too, but new personnel had recently graduated. New cadets had been trained so the protocols were needed. We had no 'Academy' to do backgrounds on our cadets, so the protocols were a necessity.

"Relax, Sergeant. I understand. I was distracted as there is a lot going on with this planet. We all have our own needs to consider along with all of it." I bit my lip. "The protocols and other procedures I lost track of," I added.

"I understand, ma'am. It has been hectic for all of us," he said. "I see you have a 'Coded Message.'" He winked, as he pointed at my computer screen, smiling, and turning to leave.

"Hang back, Sergeant, in the shadows," I commanded.

"Yes, Ma'am." He shut down his workstation and then stepped into the shadows.

Corporal Kirale came on to my ODT. "Commander, this is Corporal Kirale. We have the ship under tow. It's pretty banged up, ma'am. Power is nearly gone, and life support is failing," Kirale reported.

"Roger, Kirale, keep me posted," I replied.

"Roger, Roger," Kirale came back.

I secured the blinds and door. "Computer, secure room., Code X protocol," I commanded.

"The room is secure of all communications systems. No listening devices detected," the computer stated. Note, Sergeant Patrell remains in the room. Is security needed, Commander?" the computer inquired. "In order to proceed, Sergeant Patrell must leave the room," the computer added.

"Computer override, Protocol Five!" I commanded. "For this message, negate protocols and proceed with the message," I added. My gut was on fire concerning recent developments. I decided to play hard and go with instinct!

(STAR DATE 3-26-04/1179)

THE PASSENGER from the small ship had been taken to the infirmary and besides a few cuts and bruises, had recovered and regained consciousness. I had her brought in for questioning.

With me were Devon Margalen, Lieutenant Littrell, Seargeant Cantrell, and Jynx. I also had Anayla brought in as well. Next to this woman, Anayla was the only other human we had run into in this entire sector of space. For an area primarily devoid of life or civilization, the place was teeming, so to speak.

The 'Maker' didn't count as he had been trapped on the planet and had decided to stay behind. But Anayla and now this woman, they were 'anomoalies' as most who entered the area. From what we knew of this sector, most were usually on the run from the law, bounty hunters, or like ourselves, hiding and not wanting to be found! If they knew of each other, they may slip up or their tells may give them away.

Anayla glanced at the woman upon entry and then back at me. The woman took in the whole group, without a glance at Anayla. She took a seat across from me.

I stood up, "I hope our care has been satisfactory?" I began.

"I understand, Commander. Your soldiers have been most entertaining." The woman flashed a smile and added, "Thank you for the assistance.".

"This is an uncharted area of space. Do you mind telling us how you ended up in the shuttle in this region?" I asked.

"I imagine this does look"—, she paused, searching for words—, "puzzling?" She continued, licking her lips, "I secured passage on a freighter with no questions," licking her lips. "I imagine that's strange in your line of work?" She inquired was looking from herself, to the security detail and a glance at Anayla in restraints. "The reasons, though appearing 'strange,' are merely what was asked of me, by my employer.", she added.

"That's true. I know her," Anayla added. "More so, I know her work and what she does."Anayla smiled, looking at the enigmatic woman she added.

"Who are you?" I asked. "Let's begin there."

"Yes, introductions are part and parcel to protocol. My name is Moxie. I'm an artist, a very 'special artist,' as there is a high demand for my work," Moxie explained.

I looked at Anayla and saw she was nodding her head in agreement. "I knew of or at least had heard of this 'Moxie,'" Anayla interjected. "One of the traders, a rather rich man, had purchased a painting from her when he was a young man. He had paid a handsome price for the work," she added.

I considered it all. Just because there was an 'artist' named 'Moxie' didn't mean this woman was said person!

Almost as if on cue, Anayla began, "I know of her work because one night I was released from the slave pens and asked to join some other people to assist in entertaining. A painting was presented as a gift to the master of the household, a very expensive gift," Anayla stated. "Though that was almost a half yeardon ago, I remember it as if it happened yesterday.", Anayla laughed, looking toward Moxie.

"Yes, I remember that job. I usually don't deal with—" Moxie paused, looking for the right words before continuing, "such persons, but the offer was good, five times my usual fee, so I accepted the job. I remember you were serving the guests, slave girl.", Moxie curiously looked at the restraints, perplexed.

So there was a loose connection between Moxie and Anayla which verifies each other's stories. I considered everything I had heard.

Suddenly and unexpectedly, the Maker, teleported into the chamber. The security detail was ready to pounce, then backed down as soon as they realized, it was the old man. Anayla was surprised by the sudden appearance of him. Moxie was taken aback. Leaping out of her seat in fear, she hid behind the security detail.

"Everyone can relax. This man is with us." I commanded the group to settle down! "Though not invited to this meeting, I assume, if you appear, there has to be a good reason for it." I looked at the Maker for verification.

He simply nodded, then turned to Moxie. "I have been expecting you, though our..." He stammered for a second, looking for the right words. "Our, uhm, prior arrangement has been, shall we say, changed." He smiled at Moxie. "Everyone, please, deep breaths. This woman is in my employ as I summoned her here." He smiled.

Moxie smiled at the Maker. "You're my employer?" She seemed taken aback for some reason. The Maker stepped into the center of the room. "For the greatest work of art— 'Eve—' - I summoned the greatest artist in the galaxy to capture her in all her glory." He smiled at Moxie.

(STAR DATE 3-28-04/1179)

I CALLED another meeting summoning Lieutenant Littrell once again and Devon. I considered the 'cards in my hand', already—What I knew, what I suspected. I had formulated a plan already, but first I needed to cover some of my 'bases'!

Moxie was released from the infirmary and given her belongings retrieved from the shuttle. She met with the Maker soon afterward, and we saw little of the two. Though when someone needed information on Eve or the system, he was summoned. I also had a chat with him about the tele-transporter and establishing protocols for future events. Having people pop up all over this planet anywhere, at any time needed redress.

Moxie was covering Eve in close detail, though her activities were monitored by security. She used an old piece of tech, a '"camera."' This was certainly not something a 'spy' would employ. She didn't seem to focus on weapons systems, for example, just snapping random pics. Security continued to observe her.

I met with the team the day after and decided I'd put 'my plan' into motion and see what spawned.

Devon took a seat by the table pouring herself some nau' tea. Lyra stood by the window looking outside. She seemed caught up in deep thought.

"Could 'Moxie' be a spy or an enemy? I doubt it as she had been summoned by the Maker long before our arrival here. No one knew we were coming, and she had no idea about 'Eve,' being employed by the Maker long before we arrived!" I exclaimed.

"What was said at the meeting with her was true, all of it," Devon added. "I detected no deception from any of them. The Maker and Anayla were telling the truth," she stated.

I looked at the security report. Moxie had no modern weaponry on her. She carried a primitive two-shot derringer in her bag and nothing else. Hardly the choice of spies or saboteurs and nothing else. A few changes of clothes, the primitive camera and tools of an artist—, 'paints, canvases, brushes, - if she were a spy, she was a poor example. I chuckled at the thought. I had included all of these observations in my report before we even had this meeting.

Moxie's fumbling at the sudden appearance of the Maker was another observation. She didn't move like a trained spy or one in military intelligence. She hardly had moved like an 'athlete,' let alone one who had been trained for infiltration. Her leap from the chair and hiding behind security was more like a stumbling doddered, almost like a clumsy child who knew she was a klutz.

"I scanned the Maker, Anayla, and Moxie for anything, a second time during their sleep period. There's nothing there as their stories check out," Devon reported.

I looked at Lyra as we had heard not a peep during the entire meeting. She seemed more focused on the weather, than our discussion.

"Lieutenant?" I inquired, perplexed. "I need my best gal on this, but seems to have taken a rain check." I chuckled. The "'best gal'" remark went back to our days as young cadets; it was a pet name from back in the day.

"I checked the logs on the shuttle, and her story checks out," Littrell began. "I questioned Anayla and the Maker at depth and couldn't find a single breadcrumb," she exclaimed. "I even went into the archives and verified she is this 'Moxie', which her activities had been reported over several yeardon." She sighed.

Devon looked at her, with, - "'that look.'", - She knew as an intuitive, that something was troubling Lyra. I knew from her body language, there was something inexplicable or unobtrusive, and from Littrell's point of view, one and one was not adding up, so to speak, despite what the evidence was saying.

Littrell remained silent, so I took that moment to complete a portion of the meeting. I let the group know I was going to release Anayla. She would be given freedom as the Erai did not keep slaves!

In accordance to with our laws, she had not been proven an enemy, despite how I felt! Moxie's appearance also verified parts of her story. I had no choice but to release her training or otherwise. Slave girl or no, she was not, as far as I had observed, an enemy! If there were any 'spies or saboteurs' among us (which I suspected), I'd let them make their move as I was ready. I had many contingencies in place for such a scenario! I'd let "Moxie and Anayla" show us who they were and whose team they were on; by their actions, they would prove themselves!

"Your services are no longer needed, Counselor," I shot at Devon. "Include your conclusions in your final brief," I added.

Devon got up to leave. "Commander." She paused choosing her words carefully. "Don't go out of your way to look for 'enemies.' They'll show their stripes soon enough." She looked from Lyra, to myself and back again. "If the enemy knew what was going on here and had spies or infiltrators among us, they'd be here by now. Consider that, Commander!" she exclaimed.

Looking again once more from myself to Lyra, she smiled. "Sometimes the further away from an enemy you are, the easier it is to see them coming," she concluded. She exited the room.

I considered what she shared carefully. Devon had been a captain and had her own command at one time. She had made an error and had taken an uncalculated risk which had lost most of her crew and a ship during the Trials. Though any inexperienced captain would have made the same error, I didn't hold it against her. Her advice was wisdom grown out from experience.

I strode over to Lyra and laid a hand on her shoulder. She went at ease, exhaling deeply.

"This is me, gal, not as your 'commander,' but as your best friend. What's eating you?" I asked.

She set the cup down and strode over to the table. She poured herself a stiff glass of 'Aishrae,' an Alta(n) liquor and delicacy. It was to be sipped, but Lyra gulped it down greedily!

"You detected 'Anayla,' though not a spy or anything along those lines. This 'Moxie' is nothing like the girl," I observed. "My gut says she's clear. This 'Moxie' would be one of many who would perish, if caught on the battlefield," I added.

"I agree." Littrell nodded her head as she replied. "Though for all intensive and purposes, she passes with flying colors, and I highly doubt she is a spy or anything along those lines," she shot back. "But" something about her perplexes me?"

"But Lyra?" I inquired.

"Our enemies are the most duplicitous, canny, and organized adversaries our people have ever faced..." She looked out the window once again, hesitating. "And...",

I knew there was more to what the lieutenant was alluding.

"Is she an enemy? I sincerely doubt it, but it's just a hunch I have about her." Lyra grinned.

"Probably nothing. She was hired long before we arrived here and has passed Devon's inspection."

She pondered the thought. "Perhaps I'm just tired and paranoid." Lyra smiled as she looked at me for confirmation.

"Get some rest, Lieutenant," I commanded. " We've all been under the gun since we arrived here," I commanded.

I was with a security team. Devon Magalene, Captain Carter, Sergeant Cantrell, and Jynx were with me as the cell door opened and Anayla exited.

"The Erai do not keep slaves as that is against our customs and laws," Devon began. "In addition, you have been found innocent and not an enemy combatant, so your freedom awaits," she added.

"Since you are not a known and wanted criminal, you have full status and citizenship as one of us." Carter smiled.

Jynx handed her few belongings in a haversack to Anayla. "I'd be happy to show you around," Jynx invited her, smiling and extending her hand. "It's better than having goons shadowing you." She nodded toward the security team as she chuckled. Anayla chuckled lightly, as did Devon. Anayla took Jynx's hand and did the universal greeting of friendship

"Anayla." She grinned at Jynx.

"I'm Jynx. Pleased to meet you, Anayla," as she shook her hand.

"I'm pleased to meet you, Jynx," Anayla said in our native language. She had been learning our tongue during her lockdown, though she spoke with a deep accent.

Before they could unclasp hands, I put my own over the two. "Welcome, Anayla". Glad to have you among us. You are free to stay within the city or return to the woods. Such is our custom and tradition. Each one is to pursue their life as they see fit." I smiled. "Jynx will assist you either way," I added.

Anayla shouldered the haversack, with Jynx leading the way, she followed her out of the detention facility. Though she had been offered quarters within the confines nearby, she chose to return to the woods. Preferring the comfort and solitude of nature. I had seen this with some soldiers who had been captured by enemies and confined for lengthy periods of time; this was not unusual.

Jynx, who enjoyed nature herself, was a fitting companion for her.

(STAR DATE 4-4-05/1179)

I HAD a salvage team bring in the wreckage of the shuttle Moxie had been rescued from and was there looking over the initial report. I noticed off to one side the escape pod Anayla had used to flee the freighter. There was little evidence in the pod to help reveal whether Anayla was a spy or otherwise.

The log entry did prove the ship was a slave ship and had a cargo of new slaves. They were on their way to be sold to a trader in the quadrant Anayla had come from. Apparently, the salvage team was still going over parts of the ship, and the final report was still in the works. I looked at the logs. They still had another week to go over the pod. I'd wait.

(STAR DATE 4-7-05/1179)

I NOTICED Moxie and the Maker were always together; he was her employer. Apparently, he was going to have her make a painting of himself and Eve. I wondered how such a thing could be captured on canvas. Considering its vast size? Though I had a security team keep tabs on both of them, it appeared that Moxie was who she said she was. Images had been pulled from the the "Galactic Archives," and images had also been recovered of some of her paintings. Apparently, Moxie had done a couple self-portraits throughout her career which were on file. For all intensive and purposes, she was who she said she was. Days had passed since her rescue, and she spent time with the Maker taking photos of him as they spent a lot of time at other sites outside the Vale. She had even done some paintings during her down time. I admitted she was skilled as an artist and had talent. She had fumbled and hid behind security when the Maker had appeared and exhibited no combat skill. Moxie appeared as she claimed. She was an artist, maybe even avid explorer, but when it came to combat, she lacked and had no skill! If she were a spy or infiltrator, she was a poor example if this was what the enemy was putting out these days. I laughed at the thought, as I knew better. The enemy could be the person standing next to you, hence our precaution.

Anayla, on the other hand, took to the woods, choosing to live on the outskirts of town. Jynx, of course, provided her with whatever gear the girl asked for, though nothing extreme. The girl, if she were a spy or enemy, didn't ask for anything extreme. A few weapons anyone would take into the wilds for defense against predators, again nothing extreme. She was an enigma or wild card. Jynx stayed with her, slowly winning her confidence. Her daily reports did not reveal anything unusual.

Anayla went for walks in the woods, collecting various plants. She occasionally picked up various stones or crystals and sometimes scavenged old tech from ruins, working on some devices she made herself. She made no effort to hide or conceal what she worked on, Anayla was very forthright in her activities, being honest, sincere, and genuine from what Jynx gathered. We were both coming to the final conclusion the girl was not a spy or assassin and for all intensive and purposes, was what she claimed, a slave. Though we were both curious where she had been trained as she had skill and knew tech; one had to have been trained to acquire those skills and knowledge. But Anayla was not anxious to speak about her past, her life prior to being a slave. It would have to wait.

Anayla had taken to training in the woods. She was knowledgeable as an herbalist and skilled in collecting and processing, Jynx reported. She had also taken to helping small woodland animals and effected healing upon their injuries or nursing them back to health if they were ill or infirm. Jynx reported her animal husbandry skills, along with everything else.

There was an ancient word from the Nupandesh that described one like "Anayla," though I could not recall. It was denoted in Jynx's report, Anayla was like a "**fore-stale**, " though that was the modern slang. I recalled "**lenorades**" was the traditional translation and "**natureza**" the common in the ancient tongue of the Nupandesh! They were those who loved the woods. That put another light on the girl, a much different light. For within the Nupandesh, there were legends of the Neresturr. I shuddered at the thought, considering how the girl had been treated. They were the "Gifted"; they had innate abilities or "Gifts" that they were born with. I thought for a moment, recalling some of the teachings. There were those who worked with animals. They could connect with them and gain their trust easily over others. Animal husbandry was their gift; it came easily to them! They also had abilities to affect the weather and could communicate with the spirits of nature with ease. I would take a deeper look later. For now, something else needed my attention.

I called an impromptu meeting in the council chambers. I met with Captain Willis, Captain Carter, Commander Lisette, Dusty Rhodes, Lieutenant Littrell, Lieutenant Jensen, Sergeant Cantrell, Devon, and the Maker.

"I called this meeting to find out where we're at and the status of various missions," I began.

"Ma'am, the '***Essex*** and ***Griffon***' are ready to be launched," Lieutenant Jensen began. "***Griffon*** has her full complement of crew, but we need a command crew for ***Essex***," she reported.

"Since Lisette has a full plate, I decided I'd lend her a hand," Captain Carter began. "I have been assisting in the docks and with training. As you know, ma'am, many of our cadets are not ready for missions yet." He referred to his brief. "We've been pulling retirees from the civilian ranks, as you know. But have few with command experience." He looked my way, grinning.

I began the informal ceremony, "As you all know, we haven't had time for regular ceremonies for promotions. But this is an untraditional time. However, promotions are still called for." I grinned at the group. "Lieutenant Jensen." I looked her direction.

"Yes, Ma'am," she replied. She took to her feet, standing at attention.

"I'm promoting you to captain, I want you to take command of the ***Essex***. Lisette has assured me, you're ready.".

Lisette stepped forward, handing her new insignia and rank designation to her. Since the meeting was impromptu, I decided to do away with all the formal pomp and circumspance that would accompany the promotions.

"Sergeant Cantrell." I smiled as he rose. "I'm promoting you to Lieutenant." Captain Carter stepped forward, handing him his new rank insignia and designation.

"I want you to join Captain Jensen on the ***Essex***." I nodded in her direction.

Cantrell laughed. "I anticipated such a move and took the liberty to put together the rest of our team. We've been training together for some time." Cantrell smiled.

I smiled at him. He had been a graduate from the Academy soon after our class had left.

"That just leaves the **Intrepid**.'", I grinned, looking at Dusty Rhodes.

"Sorry, Commander," he began. "I'm old and enjoy my civilian comforts," He added. "I've seen my share of 'battle' and have had more than my fill." he bowed his head. "I don't want a 'command,' nor will I seek such!" he exclaimed.

"You were a fine 'captain,' Dusty." I pulled his record from my carry-all. "Your 'record' speaks volumes." I shook the papers in my hand, looking at him.

Dusty interrupted me, before I could go on. "Thank you, Commander. I know what my 'record' says." he paused, searching for words. "You're probably thinking about the 'Trials' and the Battle of 'Talev'." He frowned. "I don't look at those instances as some kind of example for a great 'captain,'" he exclaimed!

"But you were 'great!'", Littrell exclaimed. She got to her feet and took a knee, the old traditional form of honoring a 'Patriot.'

"Okay, settle down, everyone," I commanded. Lyra's comment took some by surprise and shocked others, seaming 'unpatriotic.'

Dusty looked at her, appalled by her comment. Then he looked back to me.

"Continue, please," I said.

"I'm not who people think I may be, despite what the 'record' says. I didn't get lucky in either of those scenarios. God had my back in those battles. You don't test the Lord thy God, a third time," He sited the Nupandesh! "I'm no, 'hero'." He sighed heavily as he sat back down.

Angry, the lieutenant left the room. I could tell she was upset.

"Meeting adjourned. Ms. Jensen, would you record the minutes accordingly?" I asked. She nodded in agreement as I turned to Devon and the Maker. "I'll meet with the two of you, later," as they both nodded in agreement.

When she wasn't training, Anayla came into town to trade for various gemstones and crystals. She had skill there as we had seen earlier which Jynx had reported on, verifying she had certain "gifts" the Nupandesh spoke of!

That put me on edge for another group of reasons beyond simple spying or sabotage! Those who had skills the Nupandesh spoke of fell into a special classification which was outside the norm. They were individuals of an epic or legendary level, - "'Lady Naneth'," who was the 'first Matron and Founder of the Erai,' is said to be one of them. 'Telaneous', who was the 'first Lore Master' who had brought the Light of Brotherhood to the Erai was another legendary person, and the 'Wordsmith'"— these people were some of those legends of which the Nupandesh spoke of. Even 'Commander Blake' and 'Shanda Du`Lock' had been entered into the Chronicles.

Whether Anayla was one of the "Gifted" or even one of the "Neresturr" was not for me to contemplate or consider.

Being at war and in unknown territory was enough on my plate as a Commander to be concerned over. Though I did find myself, curious and decided perhaps some prayer and quiet contemplation may not be a bad thing considering the circumstances. I was never the spiritual warrior big on prayer and study. Like Commander Blake or even Shanda Du`Lock, who was one of the few survivors in the battles that ensued after the time of the Trials.

I was always pragmatic, logical, and reasonable when need be. I figured if some higher power had our back, they could do their part without my meager assistance. I had a fleet of roughly one hundred and seventeen thousand souls to keep safe. This task was big enough for my capabilities and was enough to worry about. However, I decided to call counsel and with one who had the insights and understanding of which I lacked as a commander.

STAR DATE 4-8-04/1179)

I MET WITH DEVON. If anyone could set me straight regarding these spiritual concerns, it would be her! I entered, and her wry smile caught me off guard. She had something for me, but it wasn't the answers I was looking for.

"I had a feeling you'd be seeking me out for answers," Devon began. "Though my knowledge is not as extensive, as the one who trained me." She smiled as she searched my face for the answers she already knew.

"I should have known an intuitive would know what I was seeking, before I even realized what it was I was searching for," I replied, looking closer at her for some clue as to her intentions. I was puzzled.

"You are one of a few who are actually **closed** to me in certain regards!" Devon exclaimed. "Very few have that capability, but I know of a few, you being one of them," she replied.

A 'few'? I wondered.

"You are one of a few I can come to when it comes to spiritual matters. I paused, considering my words, I continued. "It's not just your gift, which has saved us countless times! You have an insight into the Nupandesh, of which I have little knowledge. I'm perplexed." I searched the room for answers. Then opening one of the blinds, I looked outside, gazing at Eve.

"I know, or at least suspect what you are looking for," Devon started, "and "there's someone who has far more insight about you and this place, you would speak with." she continued.

"About 'me', and this place?", I searched her face for clues. "Back up, you said a 'few.' Anayla?" I asked. I suspected the answer, but had to hear it from her almost for validation.

"You don't need to be validated, Commander!" Devon exclaimed. "The problem is you have closed off yourself to your own 'gifts,'" of which I sense you have several." Devon began. " Was it not your 'gut instinct,' in a certain sense, that lead us here?" Devon inquired. Before I could reply, she continued, "You think we got 'lucky' finding this refuge?" she asked once again. "There is one you would speak with, though they concern deeper teachings within the Nupandesh on the **Eyonshedar**, of which there have been only a handful." She paused. "One of legend and the other, a mere myth." Devon looked out the port window, almost looking for answers herself it seemed. "Seek out Rourke. He is here upon the planet. It is he you must speak with regarding these matters. He holds answers," Devon concluded.

One a legend and the other, a myth. I contemplated that for a minute as Devon seemed lost in thought. To my insights, talk of the 'Eyonshedar' was fairy tales! I could not place the fate of the fleet and our people's future on such trivial beliefs—, that was a gamble I was not willing to bet on!

I looked out the port hole window once again at Eve. It would turn the tide in the coming battle. Eve was the edge we had been seeking along with this planet. It was as Captain Carter had stated, why create what was 'paradise' along with such a weapon as Eve, only to abandon it?

Devon, almost sensing my thoughts, turned to me. "Speak with Rourke. He will have the answers you seek," she repeated. She reached into her pocket and pulled something out as she continued, "And he instructed me that when the time was right, I should give you this," she added.

Devon handed me a small, velvet pouch. "Rourke wanted you to have this when you were ready.

That time is quickly approaching!" Devon exclaimed.

I reached for the bag, and she clasped my hands within her own. "Open it and contemplate its meaning, after you speak with him," she added and then embraced me. I returned her hug, though it came as a bit of a shock. Devon was usually affectionate with guests and such, but never to the ship's personnel unless they were ill or shaken. Her embrace caught me off guard.

"What about Liuetenant Littrell?" I wondered.

"I'll take care of her. Leave it to me, Commander." Devon chuckled. "Doctor's orders." She smiled, and we both laughed at her comment. I was concerned about Littrell, but knew Devon could handle her.

Next to Lyra, I sure do miss, CJ and Calico. They were my 'besties.'

"One last thing, Counselor, which needs to be addressed," I asked instead of commanding. "There is a need, but I can't order you." I decided to be up-front and blunt.

Devon poured herself a shooter. Apparently she hadn't expected this. Catching an intuitive off guard was not an easy thing. She took Lyras post by the porthole window, looking into deep space.

"You're the only one left, as far as I know, that has previous command experience," I began. Before she could object, I continued. "Dusty was my only other option, and he has made it clear he will not command." I got up and took a place next to her. "Devon, we need you—, the people need you, I need you. **_Intrepid_** needs a Captain, and you're the only one left I can call upon." I sighed. I knew she could refuse as she was apprehensive when it came to commanding a ship into battle, considering her past.

Devon gulped her drink down, looking into the empty glass.

"Devon, I know about the past. But you were hopelessly outnumbered, had bad intel, and the enemy had caught us with all of our pants down during the Trials and what followed!" I exclaimed. "Dusty, Trey, Blake, they all knew there'd be severe losses. It was a gamble. They knew it, and so did we. We just didn't want to admit it," I concluded. "Despite the odds, risks had to be taken." I took her by the shoulders. "One of the most important lessons my father ever taught me was not to count the wins or losses but the outcome of the struggle." I smiled. "It's in your blood, Counselor. An 'Intuitive' as a captain? I can see the enemy running, already." I grinned, looking deeply into her eyes. "I'm asking you to believe in me, trust my instinct in making a wise choice, and you're it." I looked once again into her eyes.

"Now you're leading, not as a 'commander,' but as '**One who knows**.'" Devon smiled. "I was waiting for this moment and sought it with all my prayers," she added. "I will command, as I trust in you, Commander." She smiled and embraced me deeply.

This time I was caught off guard from her words and her actions. I pulled the rank and insignia from my pocket. "A gift for you, a fitting one at that." I laughed, and she joined me as we embraced once again.

I returned to my quarters on the ship. They seemed different for some unknown reason. Everything was in order and as I had left it. It was the vibe. I had been spending so much time on the planet, where I had private quarters along with my office. My personal quarters on **'Warbride'** seemed out of date. The crew had decorated my quarters and office down on the planet as artists, interior decorators, and such could flex their creative abilities since we now had dwellings. A number of civilians had left the ships in order to settle upon the planet and establish civilization. I had given the order and allowed them. They knew the risks but decided to live their lives and not just exist upon a ship! They took their chances like the rest of us, and I too longed for an end and a chance to just, live. Back home, I had a small place, with a garden. To retire and have time to dream and contemplate the teachnings of the Nupandesh, or life in general. Most had such dreams.

(STAR DATE 4-10-05/1179)

I WAS ready for the ride, my hovercycle on standby. I asked Captain Jensen, Jynx, Sergeant Patrell, and Anayla to join me. Jynx had reported that Anayla had probably found this "Rourke," as she had mentioned she had stumbled upon a crazy, old hermit living in a cave among the ruins. That sounded like just the man, I should talk to. I don't know why. Once again gut instinct told me, this was 'the guy'!

Sergeant Patrell and Lieutenant Cantrell pulled up with Anayla in tow. "Anayla needed some ride training, so we had to put her through the paces," Cantrell joked, a smile at the corners of his mouth.

Anayla frowned. "Put me on a horse and I'll show you how to really ride!" she exclaimed.

Jynx pulled up on her hovercycle.

Cantrell laughed deeply. "Well, ma'am, I may have to take you up on that offer soon," he said.

"We have horses that have been domesticated here on the planet." He looked at Anayla for confirmation.

"Yes, I've seen them, and they're friendly too." Anayla smiled. "Been a long time since I rode." Anayla snorted. "I enjoy riding, better than these infernal machines. Besides you can always trust a brother." She smiled deeply.

Jynx laughed, and everyone joined in. "That part right there." Jynx grinned and nodded her head, toward Anayla who smiled.

Anayla led us to the cave where she had met the old hermit. We left our hovercycles about fifty meters away, so as not to scare the old man. We parked and set off on foot for the cave entrance. I left Lieutenant Cantrell to watch over the cycles and monitor the area. He was tired as he had pulled a double shift.

Closing in on the entrance, I looked around. Something wasn't right. Once again instinct took over. Something was a miss. Our ODT were having communication and telemetry issues. It could have been a number of things, but it would have to wait. I had Anayla and Patrell take the left flank, with Jynx and Captain Jensen to my right. As we got near the entrance, from out of the bushes a huge bear or "togaranda" emerged from the brush. They were cousins to 'grizzly bears' and not to be tampered with or underestimated. They were fierce predators as their razor-sharp claws and bite could make mincemeat of an intruder quickly!

They had injured several crew members on scouting missions across the planet. They frequented caves and crags where they could nuzzle their young. Was this the right cave? The bear steamrolled Seargeant Patrell, who was closer and caught off guard by the beast's sudden appearance. The togaranda pushed him into the thicket. He was knocked to the ground from the beast's lunge. The wind was knocked out of him. He took a swipe at his leg. Anayla had enough time to dodge the lunge of the bear. She shifted to the side. Jynx was readying her flaming sword, as I pulled my sidearm, taking aim, with Jensen doing the same. To everyone's surprise, Anayla stepped forward. She had a bear skin over her head and a gemstone in her left hand, which glowed with the "Ki." She made bear-like noises, as she chanted something in an unknown language. The beast seemed mesmerized momentarily. She lunged at the bear, growling. It turned tail and dashed back into the bushes. The whole team was astounded as we had never seen a "feat" like that before.

Jynx put her sword away and helped Patrell back to his feet, making sure he was okay, as she was a trained medic. His leg had some gashes, but they were not severe as his armor had protected him from the brunt of the bear's attack. He would need treatment. Anayla put her tools away and pulled the bearskin off, returning it to her haversack. I assisted Jynx.,

"He'll be all right," Jynx assured me.

"I'm fine," Patrell muttered. He took a seat by a tree, catching his breath. Looking in the direction the bear had taken, he added, "He's lucky I was tired." Patrell scoffed as the rest of us laughed from his joke.

Anayla turned toward the bushes, as a hooded hermit

emerged. I joined her, with Jynx and Captain Jensen helping Patrell to his feet.

"You'll find my apprentice has many such abilities, and you'll need every single one, for where you're headed, Commander," the hooded figure in a serape said, as he exited from the bushes.

The old man pulled his hood down. He was wearing a sun vizor, so we could not see his eyes. He had salted hair, which was lengthy, and a shaggy beard. "I trained her well, for this mission!" he exclaimed. There was something about him. As he came closer, I studied him. I should know him, but from where?

"Sensei," Anayla said to him, as he smiled at her.

"It is good to see you again," he said to Anayla. Turning to the rest of us, he said with a broad smile, "I am, Rourke. This is my camp. Welcome." he said with a broad smile.

I got a closer look at him. He was deeply tanned and his skin ruddy from being outdoors. He had some battle scars as well. He was non-descript for the most part as he was one who would prefer solitude and not to attract attention.

"'Sensei'?" I was puzzled. We all were and taken aback by the man's sudden appearance but more so by Anayla's comment.

I had Captain Jensen take the sergeant back to the hovercycles to report our situation and tend to his injuries. Jynx stood guard outside as Rourke, Anayla and I sat down by the campfire. Rourke made nau' tea and some sawtail biscuits as we chatted.

"Anayla is your 'Apprentice'? I thought she was a 'slave girl?'" I asked the obvious. "My ship's 'counsel' had scanned her," I added, perplexed by this revelation.

"Your 'counselor' knew of specific parts of the plan as she had been cleared by me, before our plan was set in motion." Rourke grinned. But then you suspected something was amiss, did you not?" He shrugged his shoulders. We knew some of your crew had been affected by the 'mind shredders,' and others had been replaced by 'synthetics,' but we weren't sure as to who." He pulled the shades from his eyes and served Anayla and I biscuits and tea.

"And Anayla?" I knew much of what he was telling me was true as I had been warned ahead of time, hence my ruse to set the enemy up.

"Yes, I found her and her sister at a young age and began training them immediately. It was upon Talev, where we had been sent under the guise of an exploration mission. Despite being in the military, which as you know is against the Uniform Code," he exclaimed! "The 'tradition' goes, a Loremaster must approve them and train them," Rourke explained. "But after we recovered your team from Ordalia, we suspected some, if not all had been replaced by synthetics. Those very people are aboard the **Warbride** or on this planet." he shook his head as he sipped his tea.

"It was my plan, though Dusty, Trey and some of the others agreed upon it. That by putting all the suspected 'bad eggs' in one basket, would be easier to locate enemies which you yourself would be doing most of the legwork." Shaking his head he removed his serape.

"And Anayla?" I was still dazed from the girl's abilities. I sipped my tea and chomped on a biscuit as I listened.

"I had been well versed in the Nupandesh teachings and recognized Anayla's gifts immediately. Like her sister, they both excelled at their pursuits," Rourke stated. "I knew then my true calling, why I left the military," he added.

"My sister is brave. She is a great fighter, strong, confident. She had bested some of the boys of our village," Anayla explained. "It was against tradition among our tribe for a girl to bear weapons," she explained. "Long ago there were many men on our planet. There was no need for women to bear arms, so the traditions changed. Then a generation, maybe two, that would change again. There had been a conflict, and soon after that ended, a plague had broken out. Many men had perished in the conflict, and more had died in the pandemic. Like so many other villages, there were not enough hunters to gather meat and protect the village. So, my sister was selected among others who had skill." Anayla looked into the campfire as she recalled.

"It wasn't soon after, we arrived," Rourke said. "The Wyrm had an outpost on the planet that had to be dealt with. My group was assigned the task" Rourke said. "It was fate that our team was passing through the area, when we came across Anayla's village" Rourke stated. The mission had been given the designation as a 'science and exploration' expedition so as not to arouse suspicion.

There were several of these missions that had been sent out about a decade after the Trials had ended." Rourke explained.

"It was your mother who had commanded us to go. The 'Wyrm' had been sending 'synthetics' onto our home world. The civilian leadership, we learned, had been compromised, and we suspected some of the military even. You know what had been taught in history had been skewed?" Rourke asked. "It was a yaren later, maybe a little more, we 'officially' met those people who had come from that unexplored sector of space. " Rourke continued. "They had been sending Synthetics onto our home world long before we had officially met them." He frowned. "Dusty Rhodes, Commander Trey, Shanda Du`Lock and I, along with your mother, had to begin preparations for the coming conflict we knew was coming, as well as to discover more about this enemy.", Rourke recalled. "How do you fight an enemy you haven't officially met, as a people?" Rourke pondered the question.

"The Elders assigned men from the village to guide us to the outpost and assist, in dealing with it," Rourke recalled. Anayla and her sister, Flora, helped," Rourke explained. "That was when I noticed their abilities. They had to be trained." He smiled. "Disobeying orders, I began training the two immediately and others. Talev was a bone to be chewed as we soon discovered the enemies' true intentions. Dusty and the others went on to complete the rest of the mission. I chose to stay behind and be listed as, MIA, so I could continue training my students" Rourke explained. `

"It wasn't until we found that medallion that Dusty Rhodes, Trey, and I came up with the plan. It was after we had regrouped with the rest of the fleet," Rourke said. "We were not sure if the enemy knew the whereabouts of 'Eve' or not," he went on. "Remember we had picked up what was left of that crew from the downed LDL on that planet just before entering this sector? Rourke recalled. "That planet was where we found the medallion, though they did not report it" Rourke went on."

"Wait, most of my command crew, along with myself, were picked up from that planet" I explained. "What are you getting at, Rourke?" I asked.

"That was Dusty's idea—, put all the bad apples in one cart, so to speak," Rourke explained.

"Are you saying—" I began.

Rourke cut me off, "We're not sure, but we suspected some of the crew members had been replaced with Synthetics, others may have been under the influence of mind shredders" he went on. "We would have detected them if so," I explained. "Our Lore masters developed a technology to do just that." I pondered this information. "Though only a few know of the invention, which is still a prototype," I explained.

"I'm aware of that, Commander," Rourke interjected. "Dusty and Trey knew as well. The problem is these Synthetics are new, something we've never seen before" he explained. "They're more advanced, and it was learning all of this and more we came up with our plan." He continued. "We bugged your command and planted coverts to monitor the situation for leaks" Rourke stated. I'm sure you understand, Commander. We weren't sure if you had been turned or not!" he exclaimed.

"That's when we came up with the idea to have me be captured," Anayla explained. "You may not have the technology to detect them, but I can!" Anayla exclaimed.

Rourke took up the telling. "We paid a group of pirates to be 'slavers.' Only the captain and his second in command knew the truth, and then our counselor hypnotized them and made them forget." He smiled. "It had to be convincing," Rourke added.

"I see. That makes sense as we have technologies and our counselor would have caught on," I surmised.

"It was all a matter of getting captured, in a manner of speaking." Anayla took up the telling. "The only issue that came up was when the fake pirate slavers I was with came under attack. Their ship was disabled, with most of the crew abandoning ship or were killed when the ship was boarded." She explained.

"We had lost contact with her after that. We had to stick with the plan either way," Rourke explained. "Though we knew the slavers were operating in this area from our scouts and the few merchants we traded information for creds with," He added.

"How did you know we would come this way?" That perplexed me.

"We worked with the Alta(n), making many calculations. Trey, Dusty, and I, knew this region of space and the few friendly ports. There were numerous calculations that had been punched in though," he recalled. "It came down to gut instinct and common sense in the end," Rourke added.

He pulled out an old star chart and pointed to an area of space. "This area is heavily influenced by the Rogue Alliance and their allies," he revealed. "So scouts and data from our missions would have revealed that to you." He looked at me for confirmation. I shook my head.

"This area here has that space anomalies and black holes. They're in the reports," he continued.

"Yes, I remember reading about that," I replied.

He folded the map back up. "In the end, it was common sense," He concluded. "A captain gets hunches or gut instinct.", Rourke laughed.

"True." I grinned.

Anayla snorted from the exchange. "I don't know about piloting, but I know my way around the woods and how to get home." She smiled.

"Yes, Anayla, it's the same." Rourke grinned. "You fly by the seat of your pants, you develop a feel for the stars." He looked at me for confirmation.

"That and lots of hours in the simulator," I added. We all laughed.

"So Anayla, is one of the Neresturr?" I asked Rourke.

"Yes, she is, and so is her sister, Flora," Rourke explained. "It turned out there were a number of them on the planet. It was their very innate abilities that had made them develop under stress and pressure from conflict and circumstances outside their control. The Source has a plan for everyone, though such insights are not always understood or known at the time," he added.

"Where is her sister?" I asked the obvious.

"She was captured by the enemy on Ordalia, now in the hands of Leora and company, I imagine." Rourke went on. "Though she'll be safe, I was assured, though the details are not important. The enemy is fickle in the ways of Source as they see themselves superior, which makes them inferior and the way to their undoing." Rourke concluded.

I wondered if she'd be turned or replaced with a synth.

Rourke seemed to sense this. "Don't worry, Commander. The enemy senses her 'value.' They just have no idea how valuable she truly is," he explained. "Trust in the Source. Trust in yourself and instinct," he added.

Right then Captain Jensen emerged from the brush. "Our comms are having issues, ma'am." She caught her breath. "Lieutenant Cantrell took Patrell back to the Vale for treatment. We have a report from the **Repulsar**. The enemy has changed course. They're on their way here." Jensen explained.

"Then it begins." Rourke climbed to his feet as everyone assembled. We returned to the hovercycles with Rourke accompanying us.

Upon our return to the Vale, Captain Jensen and Jynx secured the hovercycles. Anayla told Rourke she needed to return to her grove, so she left, explaining she'd return shortly. Rourke pulled me off to the side.

"You would like to know about your mother and yourself, I reckon?" He searched my eyes deeply. Like Devon, if he looked at you a certain way, it felt as if he was looking through you, at your soul. Only his scrutiny was more intense! It made one squirm.

"Yes, many of the records, after the war had begun. They had been lost, and only bits and pieces were available. I know she had graduated from the Academy and the beginnings of her career in the military, but that is all."

"Your mother was one of my best students. Top in her class. I took a fancy to her quickly. She was "gifted" in many ways." Rourke smiled at the memory. "She picked my brain every moment she had available—, before class, during class, and after." He laughed. "In many ways, it was I who was learning from her, more so than what she ever learned from me" he explained. She not only had tremendous gifts but an extensive knowledge and wisdom, beyond my own," he reckoned. "She also had the highest level of life molecules I had ever seen, next to myself," He sighed.

"Go to the escape pod Anayla was in. She left something for you there. Anayla will show you, It was something from your mother. She knew this day would come and what we all would be facing. That is why she left. It was her only choice," Rourke explained. "Excuse me for a moment. There's an old friend I need to chat with. Relax, Commander, you're in good hands. We'll speak again." He smiled.

I returned to the **Warbride**. "I had been summoned to some kind of confrontation in the command section. This was unusual. Our commissioned officers never fought. They were well-disciplined, so I wondered what the uproar was about.

Captain Carter was there as he had been on station for a shift, giving some of the other crew some much-needed downtime. "It's Littrell. She had a meltdown and decided to pick a fight with some of the crew," he said.

"Is everyone okay?" I inquired.

"Nothing some more downtime or maybe even a staycation wouldn't help." Carter chuckled as he eyeballed the planet. I nodded at that comment. We had been on board these ships for some time, and our arrival here signaled to many that our journey had come to a possible end! "Yeah, she got into a bit of a scrap with some other crew, but they'll be okay," he added. "She's blowing off some steam.

I get it, considering her family and all."

"Where is Lyra now?" I asked.

"She's with Devon and Dusty Rhodes," Carter responded.

"Since you're the shift chief, I want you to take care of it, Captain. I don't want some of the crew thinking there is leniency for her discharge. I leave it to you," I exclaimed.

"I understand, Commander. Some may think favoritism as she is your best friend". I'll handle it," Carter replied.

I returned to my quarters and poured myself a drink. I knew it had to do with Dusty refusing command. Littrell had always admired him. She had since our early days at the academy. Dusty had been one of the captains that had joined with Blake during the Trials and had led his command to victory outnumbered two-to-one odds. Come to think of it, he was outnumbered three to one odds at the Battle of Talev.

It was late when we assembled for this foray to the hanger. I asked Captain Jensen and Lieutenant Cantrell along with Captain Carter, Jynx, and Anayla to accompany me. I had one of my 'premonitions' (according to Devon's explanation) long before this day. When I had received the Code X message. I decided to set my trap, and everything seemed to be playing out as I had discerned.

We pulled up to the hanger and exited the hovercraft. With me were Captain Jensen and Lieutenant Cantrell, Jynx,

Captain Carter, and Anayla a long with a security squad. We entered and found the guard station empty. This was strange and against protocol. Something was wrong? I had half the security detail go around to the back and the other half remain at the entrance.

"I'm going to have a look around," Carter said to me. Looking at Captain Jensen, he added softly, "You're with me, Jensen." he added softly. The rest of us entered the hangar storage area.

"Lieutenant Cantrell, take the left."

I looked at him. Jynx followed, readying her flaming sword.

"Anayla, this way." I saw she was readying herself. I pulled my sidearm as we took the right path.

We got up to the pod. Corporal Kirale was there.

"Took you long enough, Commander!" he exclaimed.

"Traitor!" I took aim and let fly two shots. He had a deflector shield which absorbed my blasts.

"Now is that any way to treat one of your troopers?" Kirale laughed.

"For you we'll make an exception, traitor," Cantrell said as he came around the bend, letting fly a couple shots. Jynx and Anayla were moving in, weapons at the ready. Kirale's shield absorbed the blasts, so Jynx leveled her flaming sword at him and let loose a flame bolt. His shield absorbed some of the blast, but part of it got through, but his armor took the hit.

"I told Leora, I'd deal with you personally until her arrival."

Kirale laughed. He fired a couple shots at Cantrell, who put his shield up to deflect the blasts.

"Deal with this, slag head." Jynx let loose a flame ball at the rubble Kirale was standing on, blowing it up and throwing him to the ground with rubble raining down covering him. Jynx closed and plunged her flaming sword through the rubble, knicking Kirale with it.

"Shape-shift," Jynx cried out as she tumbled off the rubble heap. Kirale stood up, throwing the rubble off. He had grown in size, now standing over twelve feet tall, and he was no longer flesh but had become an armored terror!

"Plasma grenade," I yelled as I tossed it at him. The explosion knocked him to his knees.

Cantrell took aim as he fired a couple of shots, but his armor absorbed the shots. He was rising to his feet once again.

"Oh no you don't." Anayla had pulled her weapon, a glue gun. She fired a jet of glue at his eyes blinding him, and then second shot at his feet, at the same time I tossed another plasma grenade at him. He put his hands to his face to wipe the glue away as he fell over, the explosion knocking him down.

Before he could rise once again, Jynx closed and thrust her blade, a direct hit into his chest! Kirale pushed her off. She fell away from him as he tried to get to his feet once more. I fired a couple of blasts at him, which hit his chest, as Cantrell tossed another grenade at him. He shattered into pieces from the blasts. The battle was over.

Right then Captain Carter arrived. "Every one move! The place is rigged. Go, go!" Carter exclaimed.

Anayla ran over to the escape pod and pulled something from one of the panels, as I helped Jynx to her feet. She retrieved her sword as we left.

Lieutenant Cantrell bagged part of Kirale's head and hand as everyone moved toward the exit.

We returned to the Vale.

TERMS FOUND WITHIN THE 'CHRONICLES':

Alta(n) - Mythical people from the Nupandesh. They were said to be xenophobic but helped other civilizations in times of dire need.

Ancients - It was believed they were once part of the legendary 'Mother Civilization,' which was the heart of Dominion. They have not been seen, for over one thousand years. It is believed they were destroyed in the final battle of the Ancients.

Irda(n) - The Irda had once had a thriving civilization in Dominion. They were a race of shapeshifters, they have not been seen in over a thousand years. It is believed they were destroyed in the final battle of the Ancients.

Anarue - They once had a civilization within Dominion. They have not been seen in over one thousand years. It is believed they were destroyed in the final battle of the Ancients.

Erdue - They once had a civilization within Domion and have not been seen in over a thousand years. Like the others it is believed they were destroyed in the final battle of the Ancients.

Neresturr - They are sometimes referred to as the 'Gifted.' They are individuals who have a higher percentage of 'Life Molecules' than the average person. They use their 'Gifts' which are spiritual and psychic powers for various tasks or 'feats'. They are believed to have the ability to manipulate the weather, talk to animals, control people's minds, even manipulate matter, time and space itself. Anyone who applies such abilities is said to be deploying the 'Wyrd' which is an unnatural or supernatural ability. They are trained by special teachers 'Lore masters' or other Neresturr.

Naturals - A term to describe Erai and other extraterrestrial races of the galaxy.

Metabolic State - A highly advanced meditative state.

First Place - A legendary location said to be part of the 'Mother Civilization,' though believed to be a myth and metaphorical and not literal. Also called the 'Creator' or 'Gods' home e.g. 'Heaven.' A teaching from the Nupandesh.

Mother Civilization - It was the heart of Dominion. Believed to have been a central location where the Ancients, traded and lived in peace with other civilizations, the Alta(n), Irda(n), Anarue, Erdue (for example). It is legendary and is part of the teachings from the Nupandesh.

Nupandesh - The holy texts of the Erai people.

Wyrm - The ancient enemy of all civilization. The 'Wyrm' is a monster of epic proportions and is said the devour entire solar systems like a black hole.

Minions - They are the 'Dogmen, Fiends, Mind Shredders' and other evil creatures, the Wyrm deploys to conquer enemy civilizations.

Times, Before Times - The time period of the 'Mother Civilization' and the Ancients. Also called the time of 'Dominion'.

Founder - A teaching of the Nupandesh. Also called Telaneous, who is the father of the Erai people.

Telaneous - He is mentioned in the Nupandesh. He is believed to be the father of the Erai people.

Lady Naneth - A teaching from the Nupandesh. She is believed to be the mother of the Erai people.

Word Smith - She is a legendary person said to have been the 'Eyonshedar' or super being. According to the Nupandesh there have been only two 'Eyonshedar' in the history of the Erai people. They have monstrous abilities and superpowers granted by God.

Trials - Was a civil war among the Erai people. It is believed that 'Synthetics' were the ones who started the conflict, to destroy the Erai from within. The conflict began when many with the leadership castes and military, were sentenced to death in bogus courts called 'Trials.'

ODT - 'Optical Digital Technology'. Advanced technology warn on the wrist by most Erai people, used for various tasks.

LDL - A type of Erai warship, the largest among them.

Forestal - A name for one who resides within the woods and influences animals. One of the Neresturr.

Natureza - A name for one who resides in nature and influences animals. A name for one of the Neresturr.

Lenorades - Another name for one resides in nature. A name for one of the Neresturr.

Closed - A term for someone who cannot be scanned by an intuitive / empath.

Eyonshedar - A teaching from the Nupandesh. They are said to be super beings with god-like powers and abilities.

One Who Knows - A term for one who uses their intuitive abilities to scan people or see future events.

Sun
Planet b
HD 7924
Planet c
Planet d
THE CHRONICLES OF
EVERESKA
Book IV - Discovery
Sun
Planet b
HD 7924
Planet d
Planet c
Sun
Planet b
7924
Planet d
Planet c
By Tom Cavanaugh